what the Bible
has to say about:

death

ISBN 0-687-07502-5

Scripture quotations are taken from the HOLY BIBLE, NEW
INTERNATIONAL VERSION ®. Copyright © 1973, 1978, 1984
International Bible Society.

Original edition published in English under the title
What God Has to Say About: Death by John Hunt Publishing Ltd,
New Alresford, Hants, UK.

This book was conceived, designed, and produced by

THE PALM PRESS

The Old Candlemakers, West Street
Lewes, East Sussex BN7 2NZ, UK

Creative Director: PETER BRIDGEWATER

Publisher: SOPHIE COLLINS

Editorial Director: STEVE LUCK

Designer: ANDREW MILNE

Project Editor: MANDY GREENFIELD

03 04 05 06 07 08 09 10 11 12 — 10 9 8 7 6 5 4 3 2 1

Manufactured in China

what the Bible
has to say about:

death

Mark Water

DIMENSIONS
FOR LIVING
NASHVILLE

When the perishable has been clothed with the imperishable, and the mortal with immortality, then the saying that is written will come true: "Death has been swallowed up in victory."

1 Corinthians 15: 54

Introduction For some people the fear of death haunts them from an early age. For the sick and suffering, the fear of death seems to be a dark hovering cloud, threatening to descend at any moment. The unexpected fatal car accident, or the lingering death from some malignant cancer, afflicts us with grief. Death is the familiar foe against whom no human being wins. The only things associated with death are suffering, grief, and sorrow. Yet there is a victor over death— one Christ Jesus.

So there is, for the Christian, hope. Ever since the days when Jesus walked this earth in person, his followers have believed that death is not the giant full stop that puts an end to everything as we know it. Christians believe that because Christ came alive, and is alive, his disciples will be alive with him beyond the grave. So death does not have the last word. While death may indeed be the last enemy, death is a conquered foe. Its victory is hollow. With the apostle Paul, Christians can say with conviction: "Where, O death, is your victory? Where, O death, is your sting?" 1 Corinthians 15: 55. Instead of an end we now have a beginning—resurrection life. New life ahead and new life now. Mark ends his Gospel with the death of Jesus. For Mark, death was the triumph.

Jesus said . . . "I am the resurrection and the life. He who believes in me will live, even though he dies; and whoever lives and believes in me will never die."

John 11: 25–26

contents

Part 1
The
Inevitability
of Death

8

Introduction We are born to die. In a very real sense we begin to die from the day we are born. Christians were realists about death from the first century onward. Rather than glossing over the subject, or never referring to it, as has generally been the case in so-called "polite" society, Christians were all too aware of its reality.

Death is constantly mentioned in the pages of the New Testament. The sobering fact was that one was more likely to meet an early death if one faithfully followed the teachings of Jesus than if one did not.

The Gospels record how John the Baptist spoke out fearlessly against wrong and evil wherever he found it. He did not cling to life at all costs. If only he had turned a blind eye to the scandal of the day: King Herod taking his brother's wife for himself. But no, John laid his life on the line when he spoke out against this. For his pains he was imprisoned and then beheaded by Herod.

"... you must not eat from the tree of the knowledge of good and evil, for when you eat of it you will surely die." Genesis 2: 17

Death is

Biological death is unnatural. It would appear from the opening chapters of Genesis that death was not in God's original plan. The first time death is mentioned in the Bible, it is seen as a result of human beings turning their backs on God. We view death as not only inevitable, but also as natural. It was not always like that.

unnatural

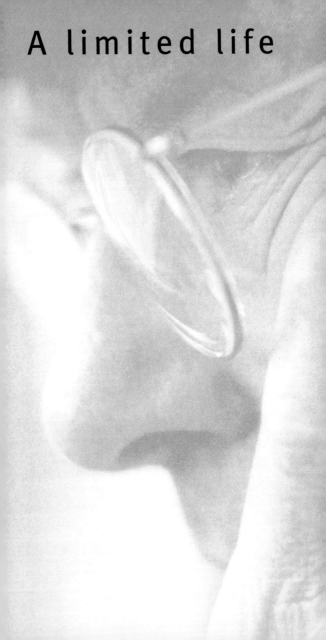

A limited life

The length of our days is seventy years — or eighty, if we have the strength. Psalm 90: 10

We must all die. We have to come to terms with the reality that we must face death. We have but a brief 70 or 80 years on this earth. The psalmist's prayer casts light on how we should live out our years: "Teach us to number our days aright, that we may gain a heart of wisdom." Psalm 90: 12.

Two who
never died

Enoch walked with

God; then he was

no more, because

God took him away.

Genesis 5: 24

But not everyone did die. Two people are mentioned in the Bible who never died: the prophet Elijah and Enoch. They were both "translated" to heaven. They never experienced the process of death, but went into the immediate presence of God in heaven. This may have been God's original plan for everyone.

Face-to-face with death

"Give me here on a platter the head of John the Baptist." The king . . . had John beheaded in the prison.

Matthew 14: 8, 10

John the Baptist lost his head for speaking out. Jesus' followers did not have some weird and wonderful notion that by some sleight of hand they would not have to face death, so long as they did what Jesus told them. No, most of them became martyrs for the Christian cause.

Jesus said . . . "when you are old you will stretch out your hands, and someone else will dress you and lead you where you do not want to go." Jesus said this to indicate the kind of death by which Peter would glorify God.

John 21: 17–19

The sentence of death

When Peter met up with the risen Christ he was given some sobering news. He was told how he would die. Tradition has it that Peter did indeed die in this way. His hands were "stretched out" as he was crucified upside down in Rome. Such early Christians met death—even martyrdom—fearlessly.

Part 2
Living in the
Light of Death

20

Introduction Once we face the inevitability of death, it is easy to become fatalists or cynics about death. If we know that death is coming to us all, we can adopt the attitude of "eat, drink, and be merry, for tomorrow we die," or we can stop believing in God because the pain of life is too great. Suffering, death, and a good God do not add up, some say.

So most people live only for this life. Christians offer the world a different viewpoint. As we live in the light of death, the idea of spending our whole lives—every minute of every day—in a quest to acquire more and more seems rather short-sighted to the Christian, although to the hedonist or humanist it may seem rather smart.

A very rich man died. During his funeral service, instead of reading, "Land *me* safe on Canaan's side," the hymn read, "Land *my* safe on Canaan's side." The preacher pointed out that this was the one thing the dead man could not arrange.

I will sing to the LORD

all my life.   Psalm 104: 33

Focus on living

Being aware of our own mortality, and being able to face the prospect of death, can help us focus on living a positive, creative, fulfilling, and unselfish life. Once we've overcome our fear of death, we have freedom to live life as it was meant to be lived: to the full, for others, and to the glory of God.

Enjoyment of life, including an appreciation of God's breathtaking creation, characterizes those who are living their lives in the light of eternity. From hearts overflowing with gratitude to God we sing:

"For the beauty of the earth,

For the beauty of the skies,

For the love which from our birth

Over and around us lies . . . "

FOLLIOTT PIERPOINT

For the beauty of the earth

The heavens declare the glory of God; the skies proclaim the work of his hands. Psalm 19: 1

Moreover, when God gives any man wealth and possessions, and enables him to enjoy them, to accept his lot, and be happy in his work—this is a gift of God.

Ecclesiastes 5: 19

"A gift of God"

But the writer of Ecclesiastes, as he portrays the meaninglessness of life lived without reference to God, has a warning that is meant to pull us up short in our acquisition-dominated culture: "He [the person who lives only for the moment] seldom reflects on the days of his life, because God keeps him occupied with gladness of heart." Ecclesiastes 5: 20.

Preparing for death: physically

Naked a man comes from his

mother's womb, and as he

comes, so he departs.

Ecclesiastes 5: 15

As we reflect on how we are but passing through this world, we may revise our lifestyle and follow one of John Wesley's mottoes:

> "Do all the good you can
> By all the means you can
> In all the ways you can
> In all the places you can
> To all the people you can
> As long as ever you can."

Living our life in the light of death can be the most positive and liberating thing we ever do. We can affirm, with the apostle James, that life is indeed but a passing mist that will quickly disappear. With that attitude to life and death, we may need to revise our priorities as we live out our remaining years.

Why, you do not even know

what will happen tomorrow.

What is your life? You are a

mist that appears for a little

while and then vanishes.

James 4: 14

Preparing for death: mentally

Preparing
for death:
emotionally

... *your strength*

will equal your days.

Deuteronomy 33: 25

People who live their lives conscious of God's presence seem to have the happy knack of being able to "let go" of their attachment to people and possessions, and yet at the same time to be even more caring and loving. Their "strength" does indeed equal their days, as their "strength" comes from their trust in the Lord.

Preparing
for death:
spiritually

"Do not work for food that spoils, but for food that endures to eternal life."

John 6: 27

The spiritual dimension is not the only dimension to life, but it is the one that is supposed to influence and color our whole approach to our short stay on this earth. Strangely, those who are most heavenly minded prove to be those who are of most earthly use.

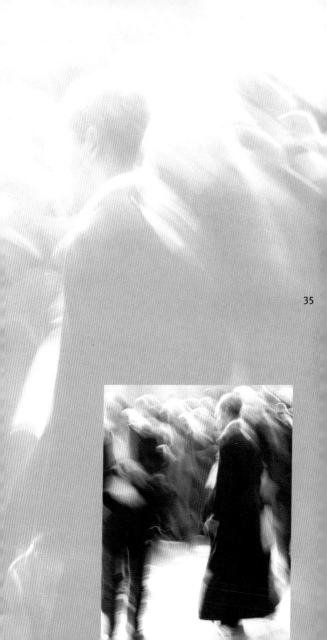

Part 3
Jesus and
Death

36

Introduction In Jesus' day, death was viewed in the light of the classical writers, who had only a grim and depressing view to express. According to Aeschylus, "Once a man dies there is no resurrection." Theocritus agreed: "There is hope for those who are alive, but those who have died are without hope." One classical epitaph read: "I was not; I became; I am not; I care not." In response to this, and in line with Jesus' teaching, the apostle Paul could write, "If only for this life we have hope in Christ, we are to be pitied more than all men." 1 Corinthians 15: 19.

So Jesus brought a revolutionary view of death. Death was no longer viewed as the end. Jesus taught that eternal life is God's gift for the here and now, and that it extends into the hereafter. The English novelist and author of *The Water Babies*, Charles Kingsley, put it this way:

"It is not darkness you are going to,

for God is Light.

It is not lonely, for Christ is with you.

It is not unknown country, for Christ is there."

Jesus brings

Jesus did not avoid speaking about death, but his message majored much more on the theme of life. The life he spoke of was the life that had conquered death. The life that Jesus promised was spiritual life. This is the kind of "full" life that his first followers experienced as they left everything to follow him.

"I have come that they may have life, and have it to the full." John 10: 10

life

A surprising funeral

Jesus called out in a loud voice, "Lazarus, come out!" The dead man came out . . ."

John 11: 43, 44

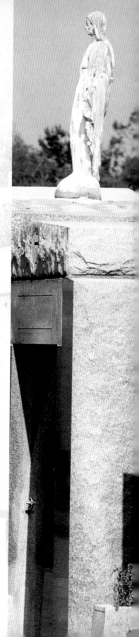

When Jesus arrived at the graveside of his friend Lazarus, he was met by Mary and Martha. They loved Jesus and shared their grief with him over their brother who had been dead for four days. Jesus confronted death head-on and brought back Lazarus from the dead. That gave the two sisters a new outlook on death!

"Young man, I say to you, get up!" The dead man sat up and began to talk, and Jesus gave him back to his mother.

Luke 7: 14, 15

42

Life from

Lazarus was not the only person Jesus raised from the dead. Jesus once met a sad funeral procession outside the town of Nain. The chief mourner was the mother of the young man they were about to bury. It was doubly sad as she was already a widow. Filled with pity for the mother, Jesus brought her son back to life.

the dead

Jesus' resurrection

If you went around pre-Christian tombs in Palestine, you would find no signs of hope for life after death. But now if you go into a Christian cemetery, the grave-stones are engraved with texts about the resurrection and heaven, and hope for peace in the afterlife. So, why the difference? Put simply, it is because of Jesus' own resurrection.

"He is not here; he has risen, just as he said. Come and see the place where he lay." Matthew 28: 6

Jesus said, "For judgment
I have come into this world,
so that the blind will see
and those who see will
become blind." John 9: 39

Judgment

day

Down the centuries, one of the main reasons people have feared the prospect of death lies in their worry about judgment. Will we be judged after we are dead? Jesus never minced his words about judgment. He said that he had come to judge people. While he mainly emphasized that he had come to bring them spiritual life, he never soft-pedaled judgment.

Comfort for the dying

We need to think of heaven much more than we do. That is one of the best ways to gain spiritual strength as we face death. In heaven, "There will be no more night. They will not need the light of a lamp or the light of the sun, for the Lord God will give them light. And they will reign for ever and ever." Revelation 22: 5.

66

Comfort in grief

Praise be to the God and Father of our Lord Jesus Christ, the Father of compassion and the God of all comfort, who comforts us in all our troubles, so that we can comfort those in any trouble with the comfort we ourselves have received from God.

2 Corinthians 1: 3, 4

If we have ever experienced God's comfort ourselves, then it is with this same comfort that we are to endeavor to bring God's comfort to other people in their sorrow. God comforts people through people. We are to rejoice with those who rejoice, and weep and mourn with those who weep and mourn.

We believe that Jesus died and rose again and so we believe that God will bring with Jesus those who have fallen asleep in him.

1 Thessalonians 4: 14

What about the

The recent Christian converts at Thessalonica wrote to the apostle Paul asking him about their Christian loved ones who had died. Would they miss out when Jesus returned at the end of the world? Paul tells them: "Brothers, we do not want you to be ignorant about those who fall asleep." 1 Thessalonians 4: 13. Jesus will bring them with him.

Christian dead?

Brothers, we do not want you to . . . grieve like the rest of men, who have no hope.

1 Thessalonians 4: 13

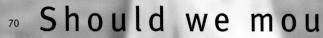

Should we mou

Of course, as Christians we should give full expression to the deep and lasting sadness we feel on the death of a loved one. But, says Paul, we should not live in despair or act like those who do not have hope in the resurrection and the afterlife with God.

?

Part 5
After Death

Introduction Today most people avoid all sight of death and never wish to peer beyond the grave. Rather, the finality of death is concealed in euphemisms and sentimentality. In place of coffins, we now have "caskets," the mortuary has become a "chapel of rest," and the dead are "the deceased."

The following radio commercial used to be aired, sung to the tune of "Rock of Ages"!

"Chambers' caskets are just fine,
Made of sandalwood and pine.
If your loved ones have to go
Call Columbus 690.

If your loved ones pass away,
Have them pass the Chambers way.
Chambers' customers all sing:
'Death, o death, where is thy sting?'"

Christians feel greatly privileged to be able to express at Christian funerals their "sure and certain hope" in the resurrection life. They love to echo the words of John Newton's hymn "Amazing Grace."

"When we've been there ten thousand years
Bright shining as the sun,
We've no less days to sing God's praise
Than when we've first begun."

When the perishable has been clothed with the imperishable, and the mortal with immortality, then the saying that is written will come true: "Death has been swallowed up in victory."

1 Corinthians 15: 54

Death has always been the great stumbling block for human beings. But now everything has changed. Death is defeated; we can celebrate the death of death. Yes, we still die, but because we have eternal life, everything has changed. This eternal life starts in the here and now and continues through death, so we remain spiritually alive, forever.

Death of death

After this I looked and there before me was a great multitude that no one could count, from every nation, tribe, people and language, standing before the throne and in front of the Lamb. Revelation 7: 9

76

Who goes to heaven?

John Newton, the writer of the popular hymn "Amazing Grace," once wrote: "When I get to heaven, I shall see three wonders there. The first wonder will be to see many there whom I did not expect to see; the second wonder will be to miss many people who I did expect to see; the third and greatest of all will be to find myself there."

Do all go to heaven?

For I take no pleasure in the death of anyone, declares the Sovereign Lord. Repent and live! Ezekiel 18: 32

What about those who have never heard the gospel? Are they condemned to hell? What we know about God is that he is totally loving and completely fair. He will judge us on the opportunities we have had in life and on the amount of light we have been given. There will be no mistakes in heaven.

80

Will we know
our loved ones?

Heaven
and hell

**"You snakes! You brood
of vipers! How will you
escape being
condemned to hell?"**

Matthew 23: 33

*Do we still need to talk about
heaven or hell? Jesus talked more
about this topic than anyone else
in the Bible. "But then," comes
the reply, "he was a child of his
times." In one sense, Jesus was
that, but more importantly he
was the Son of God. So we note
what he said, even about hell.*

Does hell really exist?

For God did not send his Son into the world to condemn the world, but to save the world through him.

John 3: 17

Who still believes in fire and brimstone, and hapless souls dangling over the pit of hell? This is a very serious subject. Jesus spoke about hell as well as heaven. Nobody can go to hell unless they deliberately scorn God's love. Our choice may be for hell, but God's choice is for us to go to heaven.

What about babies?

Then little children were brought to Jesus for him to place his hands on them and pray for them . . . Jesus said, "Let the little children come to me, and do not hinder them, for the kingdom of heaven belongs to such as these." Matthew 19: 13, 14

God is both loving and just. Babies are too young ever to have had the opportunity of rejecting God. We can rest assured that Jesus' loving embrace awaits all babies who die. God welcomes everyone who does not reject him. That is his nature.

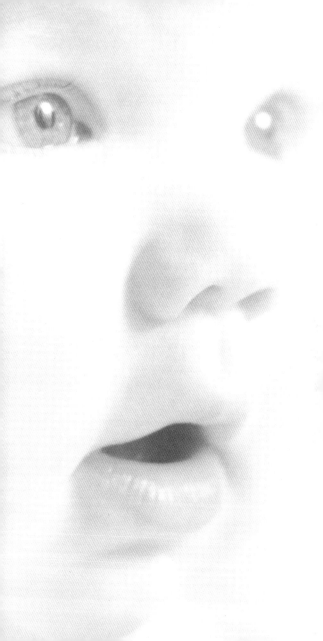

"Do not store up for yourselves treasures on earth . . . But store up for yourselves treasures in heaven."

Matthew 6: 19, 20

Jesus on heaven

Jesus likened heaven to treasure. Earthly treasures are all fatally flawed. They fail to give total and lasting satisfaction, no matter how dazzling and appealing they appear to be. Lasting treasure for which all people long is only found in heaven, in Jesus, in God.

Part 4
Dying Well

Introduction Our approach to death, and the way in which we face death itself, will be governed by our beliefs. During World War II the German theologian and pastor, Dietrich Bonhoeffer, who had once been a pacifist, joined in an unsuccessful plot to assassinate Adolf Hitler. The last moments of his life were recorded by the prison doctor:

"Through the half-open door in one room of the huts I saw Pastor Bonhoeffer, before taking off his prison garb, kneeling on the floor praying fervently to his God. I was most deeply moved by the way this lovable man prayed, so devout and so certain that God heard his prayer.

"At the place of execution, he again said a short prayer and then climbed the steps to the gallows, brave and composed. His death ensued after a few seconds. In almost fifty years that I worked as a doctor, I have hardly ever seen a man die so entirely submissive to the will of God."

58

The cords of the grave coiled around me;

the snares of death confronted me.

Psalm 18: 5

The cords of death

It's one thing to think in the abstract about death; it's a totally different proposition to come face-to-face with death. Anyone who trusts in God, like the psalmist, finds it possible to place his or her trust in God. "In my distress I called to the LORD; I cried to my God for help." Psalm 18: 6.

Advantages
of death

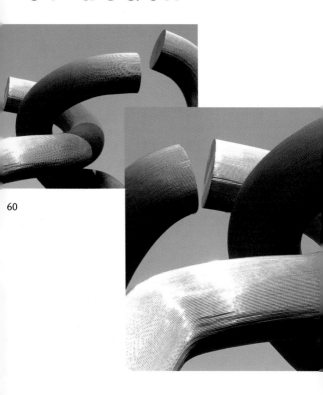

I am torn between the two: I desire to

depart and be with Christ, which is better

by far. Philippians 1: 23

As Paul lay in prison, chained to a burly Roman soldier, he mused about death. It was no academic or philosophical game for him. He expected to be beheaded any day. With such thoughts in mind, he wrote his letter to the Philippians. Yes, he concludes, being with Jesus, after we are dead, is best of all.

Therefore we do not lose heart. Though outwardly we are wasting away, yet inwardly we are being renewed day by day.

2 Corinthians 4: 16

As we grow older and our bodies and even our minds begin to deteriorate we feel we are losing a grip on life. Often we feel depressed and afraid. Yet Paul is full of hope. There is more to a human being than a body and a mind. Though physically weak, we are spiritually invigorated.

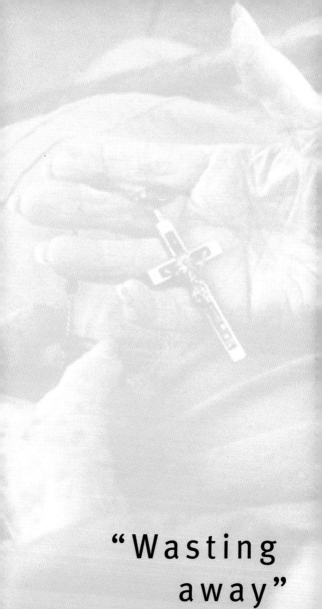

"Wasting
away"

"He will wipe every tear from their eyes. There will be no more death or mourning or crying or pain, for the old order of things has passed away."

Revelation 21: 4

After that, we who are still alive and are left will be caught up together with them in the clouds to meet the Lord in the air. And so we will be with the Lord forever.

1 Thessalonians 4: 17

It is quite natural for us to want to know if we will recognize our Christian loved ones who die before us. We will. They will be there with the Lord. On the Mount of Transfiguration the disciples saw Jesus talking with Moses and Elijah. They were real and recognizable people.

N. D. E.

The other criminal . . .

said, "Jesus, remember

me when you come into

your kingdom." Jesus

answered him, "I tell you

the truth, today you will

be with me in paradise."

Luke 23: 40, 42, 43

Near-death experiences are fascinating. Do people have a glimpse of heaven in their out-of-body experiences? The gap between life and death is such uncharted territory. It is hard to say anything for certain in this area. But Christians do know that when they die they will be with Jesus.

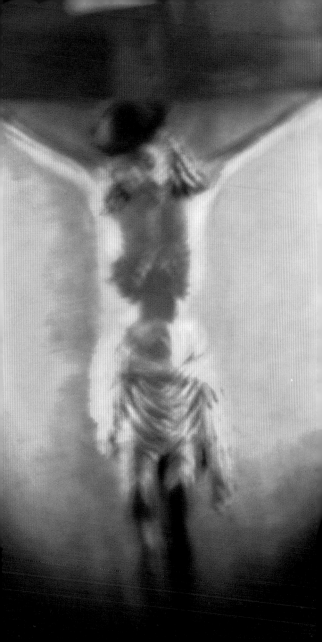

It seems so harsh to imagine that a loving God will not welcome everyone into heaven. But if we choose to reject God and turn down his offer of love and forgiveness, it is then not so much a matter of God being unkind to us, as of our willfully spurning his loving overtures.

God . . . wants all men to be saved and to come to a knowledge of the truth. 1 Timothy 2: 3, 4

What about unbelievers?

A glimpse of heaven

In a loud voice they sang:

"Worthy is the Lamb, who was slain,

to receive power and wealth and wisdom

and strength and honor and glory and

praise!"　　　　　Revelation 5: 12

The best place to find out about heaven is in the last book of the Bible, where John spends 22 chapters setting out for us in the book of Revelation his many visions of heaven. It is full of symbolic imagery. In heaven the living Lamb, who had been killed, is being worshiped by an innumerable congregation of believers.

A heavenly dwelling

We . . . would prefer to be away from the body and at home with the Lord. So we make it our goal to please him, whether we are at home in the body or away from it.

2 Corinthians 5: 8, 9

When history ends, heaven and earth will be one.
Then God's dwelling will be with men. We say that
when Christians die they go to heaven. While
accounts of heaven may use symbols, they convey the
truth. Heaven is not so much a place that can be
located above the sky, as Jesus' immediate presence.
We can be in heaven on earth.

We have heard of your faith in Christ Jesus . . . the faith and love that spring from the hope that is stored up for you in heaven.

Colossians 1: 4, 5

For Paul, life here on earth was but a small part of the whole of life. He often had his eyes trained on the life to come. One of his favorite topics was eternal life. This, he explained, was the spiritual life that came from God as a gift. It was the basis for his hope of knowing Jesus face-to-face in heaven.

I press on to take hold of that for which Christ Jesus took hold of me . . . I press on toward the goal to win the prize for which God has called me heavenward in Christ Jesus.

Philippians 3: 12, 14

What really matters

We might have thought that by the end of his life Paul would have been content to sit back and feel that he had no more to do, so far as his own Christian life was concerned. After all, he had been a much-persecuted pioneer missionary. But no, the one thing Paul did was to press on to know Jesus better—and the culmination would be heaven.

He has given us new birth into a living hope through the resurrection of Jesus Christ from the dead, and into an inheritance that can never perish, spoil, or fade—kept in heaven for you.

1 Peter 1: 3, 4

It seems rather strange that Christians say that they are happy to be living in the shadow of death. But for us, death is a mere paper tiger. It holds no fears. Rather, we are more happy than we can say, because we are already living in the light. We have a secret inheritance awaiting us. We cannot wait for heaven and to be with Jesus.